Still Some
Cake

Books by James Cummins

The Whole Truth
Portrait in a Spoon
Then and Now
Jim and Dave Defeat the Masked Man
  (with David Lehman)
Still Some Cake

Still Some Cake

James Cummins

Carnegie Mellon University Press
Pittsburgh 2012

Acknowledgments

The American Poetry Review: "This Night of All Nights"
The Antioch Review: "Freud," "Tiresias"
Best American Poetry Blog: "Mad Men"
The Colorado Review: "Buying a Dog for Margaret"
The Dark Horse: "The Snipers," "The War of All Against All"
Jacket: "The Poets March on Washington"
The Journal: "My Father's Hair"
LIT: "Sporting Life"
The Paris Review: "The Passion"
Praxilla: "The Pursuit of Happiness," "Washing the Dimes and Nickels"
The Western Humanities Review: "Moses," "Wars of Nutrition"

Best American Poetry 2005: "The Poets March on Washington"
Best American Poetry 2009: "Freud"

Book design: Victoria Adams

Library of Congress Control Number 2011926145
ISBN 978-0-88748-545-9
Printed and bound in the United States of America

10 9 8 7 6 5 4 3 2 1

Contents

IV.

V.

VI.

I

This Night of All Nights

i.

When you live in a small city in the Midwest
the late evening air can smell sweet
as you stand in the middle of an empty parking lot
after a meal of country-fried chicken and mashed potatoes.

And if you take a certain road home
you can almost believe you're in West Virginia,
driving the curving two-lane asphalt
among the hillsides and trees and young deer.

The people in the houses along the road mostly come
from West Virginia, or Kentucky, or Tennessee,
and they watch their televisions every night,
having seen enough stars to last a lifetime.

When you live in a small city in the Midwest
it's easy for the night to tell you
you are nothing and have no meaning
and should hurry home to your family.

ii.

I wake and a fragment, a wisp
entices, then disappears into the forest
of an earlier time, and I am left
in a clearing where the sun is stale

or the moon is not a pretty wafer,
and the day long ago when colors
were sounds, and sound a masterpiece
of color and form, recedes again
into dream forests, crosshatchings.

You lifted the dish with the melted cheese
for the soufflé you never touched,
being three martinis to the good already
at a lunch that comes clear again
in the forest, briefly—radiant eyes trapped
in the woods of your three companions,
who just want to laugh and love you.
You say again, in this memory-forest,
"I hope you won't tell R—" then raise
the enormous ladle, using it like a spoon,
and that is your lunch, three martinis
and a dish of lukewarm melted cheese.

Your eyes look like a four-year-old's
who sees something he wants and takes it.
And I love you for this gesture though
I'm old enough to see the forest I'll enter
soon, the one you will be leaving, knowing
so much more than I of its bewilderment.
The gesture—willful, cold as it is warm—
admits the friendship of us three, even
as we stand beyond, untouched, not privy yet
to the nightmare of too many fragments,
pieces of dreams left ragged on branches,

when the muse abducts you, carries you
through word-forests, forests of words.

iii.

All men have some fantasy or other about the boots.
Some want them left on; some want to take them off.
Some want the boots to march into them, victorious.
If you want them left on, she'll lie under you;
she'll let you use the uncomfortable to assert
the primacy of the morning, your wild life of the senses—
dark, unimaginable, but mounted.
If you want them to march into you, the same,
only reversed, you underneath, applauding,
edges accepted willingly, O willingly!
I like to take them off; I like to remember the body.
I like to remember there is a secret that led her
to put them on, the boots; that she'll share it with me
if I don't assume I know it.

iv.

I wake on the edge of knowing
something. Earlier a word had eluded me,
so I put its friends in a lineup—
Number 3, please step forward—No,
under the light it's none of these—
and what wakens me is the remnant
of the fear of losing my mind combined
with the heavy-duty agitation of the beef

brisket sandwich I had for dinner,
which I can smell in my urine as I piss.
As usual, I'm the victim of inchoate fear
that, in the light, I'd take the rap for,
indulged in like the beef brisket sandwich
over my wife's offer of potato latkes—
and that's the word, by the way, *indulge*—
I'd asked my daughter and her friend
to pull their hoods over their hair wet
from the pool as we came out into the night air;
and when they demurred, in their eleven-year-old
immortality, I'd wanted to say, *Indulge me*—
indulge your cranky over-cautious father,
but could only find *pacify, placate,*
so lifted the hoods over their skulls myself,
searching for the word all the way to the car,
until indigestion and the fear of Alzheimer's—
and something else, something more elusive—
wakes me in the cold panicked certainty
that the *aluminum zirconium* in our bodies,
facilitated by the aerosol spray refined by
Robert Abplanalp in 1948, the year of my birth,
is the direct cause of the rise of dementias
in this here life in these here United States.
I lie for a few minutes as the panic subsides,
hoping for a return to sleep—it's four a.m.—
but I need to expel a beef-laden pee,
and the nagging almost-knowing causes me
more alarm than I admit. I promise myself
I'll research *aluminum zirconium* tomorrow—

today—maybe find a baking soda roll-on,
though the murk of Armand Hammer's
connections to the Nazis—I'm being funny
now, "indulging" myself because the act
of writing this has soothed me, indulged me,
eased me past the raw edge of the almost-knowing,
until I could put it in the frame of my attempts
at logic, keep its painfulness at bay. Who
doesn't do this, in some way shape form,
though that's no excuse, and all excuses
are a way of living, a way of wasting time.
My wife offered me latkes and salad,
and I turned her down. Who can say
what holds a marriage together,
the logic of it, why we are vulnerable
to dreams, and almost know.

V.

My eighteen-year-old daughter—
my Katherine, my light—
comes home from school for the weekend
and watches a movie

in "my" room, the room
where I sleep, alone,
and where the family gathers,
when it gathers,

to watch TV.
She's rented a movie from Blockbuster,
a serious one,
The Ice Storm, and because

I'm taking her sister, Margaret,
and Margaret's best friend, Maddy,
swimming in the indoor pool
at the university gym,

I blunder in on what
at her age I would have called
the nearest thing I know
to religious experience:

watching a serious film.
I need my gym bag,
wallet, and the basketball I bought
so Margaret could practice;

my rummaging interrupts
the spell of the movie,
and when she asks me
what I think of it,

I know it's partly awkwardness,
and partly she values my opinion,
and partly she can't stand surprise,
never could, my sweet

serious first-born whose
carefree attitude hides
death-loyalty to her friends
and a fierce sense of justice.

So like a fool I tell her
I taught the book once
and so loathed the "Christianity"
of its author the memory

even now is like indigestion
from a beef-brisket sandwich;
and she asks me who dies
and I tell her that too,

thinking this moment is about us,
father and daughter, friends,
and not about her own
mind groping with what

I've groped with all my life, too.
I've intruded on this
and ruined the power
the art, good or bad,

might have achieved.
She doesn't know this; or rather,
the ways we stunt each other
are deflected deep

into the body, the mind;
and I'm sorry for this,
and don't know how to redeem it,
except to write this down.

vi.

I wander through "the American night";
I'm out again, getting food.
I remember, long ago,
wanting to say something about the buildings,
how their empty windows were like eyes.
Even then I knew
the nostalgia of such statement,
yet the overcrowding persisted, the number
of empty windows like eyes wandered
through the night of me, unsaid.

The neon is like a trick we have mastered
or a pet who surprises only
by the depth of our emotion.
The neon is like a pet,
a comfortable welcome.
In youth it's a normal desire
to seek the meaning behind each thing,
or equally, to reject all meaning.
It's all how we teach life
to welcome us hospitably.

I wander through the American night,
the night of voices, broken hips,
the hum of neon formed into friendly words.
In youth it's a normal desire.
The neon is like a pet.
The hum and tubing of voices
cry out above the hips, broken and unbroken,
from buildings with empty windows like eyes.
We teach life to welcome us.
Even then I knew.

vii.

Because you were beautiful, and because
once, in early evening light, you stood,
head down, across from me on Calhoun Street,
then looked up, and made a furtive wave,
and looked down again, I married you.

viii.

Need drives us to the door
of each other. *Don't open. Don't open.*

"You are the tall drink
of water I parch for."

"I can see into you;
you can't." This is not

reason to open. *Open
the door. O please open.*

ix.

A man walks into the kitchen.
He is angry at his own despair.
In this way, he is not unlike his wife's father.
Perhaps he is even growling a little,
the way the older man would sometimes do,
stalking through a room.

His wife was expecting her husband.
This appearance of her father unnerves her.
She is making fettucine. She says,
"I'm *almost* finished with this—I *said*
I'm almost finished with this!"
Her voice is small, afraid. And angry,
at the fear her father's voice
awakens in her—the fearful memory
of her arbitrary father, all fists.

Her husband puts some ice in a glass.
"You don't have to *say* everything,"
he says. "You can be quiet. Your family
says whatever comes into their heads."
He is thinking, *I can't stand it.
Thirty years of being her father.
I can't stand it anymore.*

His wife is tired from working all day.
She has drunk too much wine. She says,
"Everything that comes out
of your mouth about me
is terrible and mean. Everything
you say about me is mean."
She walks into the dining room.
The husband carries the bowl of fettucine.
They sit down in silence.

Their daughter has gotten an A on a test;
she is happy with the glow of reward
for hard work. Her father thinks,
Thank goodness my daughter is only herself,
not someone else.

The woman begins to weep softly.
"What's wrong, Mommy?" the daughter asks.
"Why are you crying? Daddy,
why is Mommy crying?"

The man feels like a little boy.
It's all too much for him.
"It's okay, sweetheart," he says to his daughter.
"Everything's okay." He smiles.
"Hey, let's show Mommy that test."

The mother wipes her eyes.
"I'm all right," she says, and smiles.
"Everything's all right."

X.

Eliot searched for the booth of light
in which the cosmic quiz show
asked its one continuous question.
He stood in the eternal silence
just before speech, knowing the answer.

Some personalities seek
the end of an inner garrulity,
the moment when talk is irrelevant,
when seeing becomes a form of hearing,
and hearing itself is blessedly relieved of sight.

It's in that moment we exist.
You can say neurotransmitters fire
that never fired before, or the snake
of the spine has made it all the way
to the skull cavity where its skin

sloughs off, revealing the illusion
of the skin, the illusion of the blossom.
You can say synapses are firing,
blazing like fireworks off a barge
where six or so men, half-naked

and sweating, are working in silence
under the glare, and the lacework designs,
and the smoke, and the distant cheering.

You can say they are efficient, content.
You can say what you want.

xi.

You are the seer of far markets, bazaars;
also, you're in the grip
of caressing your own face, head,
your own lips beginning to yield.

What's the reality
behind the fields? The fields.
Right? Hello?
Right?

The courthouse greens.
Mid-afternoon, summer blurs the trees
with its thick breath,
its thick smoky breath.

I've spent the day staring
at the window.
I lift it up; suddenly,
it's evening.

xii.

Not all of us should rage against the dying
of light that, after all, still lights the way
for those who follow us. When rage transcends,

becomes a purified response to death,
affording some among us a way out—
all hail the God of Rage, then: we can say
good-bye to stalwart types with a salute!
But when rage isn't how we see the world—
its fire not the core of our own being—
it's wrong to offer Death a hollow core.
The masks we make to mask our loneliness!
When some old man won't bless his son, the son
then blesses him, and swears *he* has been blessed.

xiii.

I turn on my TV: a blue fretwork
like the interior of a diamond
or the cathedral of a glacier's blue light
holds prisoner replicants who look "like us"—
though in a galaxy we haven't named.
A scene ensues, of a most manly delight:
the leader calls a challenger "snot-nose."
He's nailed the young buck's narcissism dead
to rights, but then some other creatures show,
who are all teeth, demanding fealty.
The leader now is made to kneel before
the dentally deranged one's "Wand of Force."

I flip on CNN, its fake logic
at least the clay from which my spine's been formed.
I think there's still some cake in the kitchen.

xiv.

God is weakness, the inability
to draw deep breath
because you've been unkind,
a future cul-de-sac
you hurtle toward, heaving
the carapace of your chest.

There is no meaning
until meaning is everywhere
singing in the voices
of the most casual requests
and the most urgent:

an old friend's message
to call him back,
a daughter's desire to sit
with you during a movie,
a wife's cry
from the drink-blunted moment
not to be alone,
this night of all nights.

II

Washing the Dimes and Nickels

I saw them stacked on the washer, debris
from previous loads: dimes and nickels.
I folded the towels that lay in the dryer,
transferred the wet load from the washer,

put a new one in, and reached for the stack,
before I headed back up the stairs;
but the coins were sticky to my touch,
coated with liquid soap. I carried them

into the small bathroom off the kitchen,
washed them, nickel by nickel, dime
by dime. Usually, I think of them as tiny,
but now they were large in my hands,

like small plates. I rinsed each to the rim,
thumbing soap from the center to the edge,
and laid them out to dry along the sink.
Then I felt foolish for the care I'd taken:

had their small value been worth my time?
There was a fraudulence about them,
these nearly worthless images from the past;
perhaps I should have thrown them

in the garbage like any other pile of junk.
My wife's mother died this past week;
my father, a year ago; her father, five.
We paid strangers a lot of money to wash

their bodies, prepare them for the grave.
They had become extraneous, unnecessary,
even to our higher-valued bodies which
still bore some relation to our worth.

My Father's Hair

i.

My father always tried to see meaning;
this was a comforting thing.
It suggested there was a point to it all,
if only one could find it.
It gave a son something to do,
making sense of Garner Ted Armstrong,
on long drives back from the track,
or retrieving dice he rolled
endlessly, on Sunday afternoons,
noting the combinations on a pad,
in the bedroom, among the stacks
of yellowing *Racing Forms.*

My father locked me in a closet once,
for a joke. His mother had done it to him,
and even as a child I knew his laugh
was like her laugh as she'd walked away,
ignoring his frantic pounding
in the dark. I also knew
he hadn't liked the way he felt,
laughing that laugh, and he'd rushed
back to let me out, and I could see
the shame all over him, the dirty laugh.

My father still comes to me in dreams.
I don't discourage this.

I don't tell him, no, it's time
for you to rest, to go wherever
those of you in death will go.
I admit that I don't know.
And perhaps it isn't only my dream;
perhaps I've wandered into his.
It makes sense when you think about it:
I wasn't the meaning my father
was searching for, and I knew this
as a child. What if he comes back

to make amends? Or what if it turns out
I've summoned him, to make my own?
We don't have to know everything.
In this dream he wears a yellow shirt.
An old girlfriend of mine, Paula Ashbrook,
once said to me I was a "good bet"
because my father was "a dreamboat."
In the dream he looks like a man
a woman would find attractive.
I never dream about my mother.

My father is thinking about something.
We're in some sort of gymnasium,
but whatever game is going on
is at my back. My father sits
high up, in the top row, in fact;
he is searching intently for meaning.
He isn't young, but he's in his prime;
his famous hair is combed back.

I know he'll see me, and he does,
and waves, and it's the right distance:
everything that's between us
can come into our eyes.

ii.

My father combed his hair straight back,
thick black straight hair, not like
the curly brown I inherited from my mother.

Even at 80, white and dirty-gray,
his hair was thick, a sign so many women
look for, according to my mother.

I tease her: You mean *you* looked for!
And for a minute she's a girl again,
my father's hands tangling her curly hair.

My mother didn't lie to anyone,
I've come to understand. She hoped
anticipating what they'd need

and giving it to them before they knew
to ask would make them all, and her,
happy. I've never understood her pain,

the way I understood my father's.
I never dream about my mother.
But all that's useless now. He's dead,

and her long-suffering abiding of his needs
changes back into that first love of his hair.
I miss him, too, and missing can release

a sudden memory, the early days of a son
watching a father take care of things:
pissing in the toilet each morning, shaving,

teaching me how to clean the garage,
as if it were a punishment, my mother's
fingers running through his thick straight hair.

We forgive them when they leave us
only if the thread of love is never broken,
however strained and thin it can become.

I shave. People say I look more and more
like my father. I comb my hair straight back,
trying to catch a glimpse of him in the mirror.

Old Story

Abraham

At morning Abraham awoke,
yet felt a difference as he walked
among his villagers, though he
couldn't explain: he knew they were
his people still, yet they were not.

Something had happened in the night,
some dream he couldn't remember.
Or maybe this was all to do
with the strange guests at dinner—
weary travelers, he had thought,

weary desert travelers to whom
one must show the courtesies:
water, of course, much water,
for bathing as well as drink; figs
in milk, and bread, lamb; and wine.

They'd eaten with spirit, and gratitude;
they had eaten as men eat
at home, fully, tearing the bread;
yet with an added grace—even,
he might have said, an affection.

There had been a moment, just the one,
but remarkable—amazing, even—

could the old man but credit it:
the one who spoke, the one on whom
the others seemed to wait,

reached for something, wine perhaps,
and Abraham was sure he saw
a light dispense the colors
of the spectrum, as a prism
disperses its divided light;

and the arch of the stranger's form
somehow did not make sense
to the old man, but seemed—
it was the wine, of course—
it seemed almost not human;

for a sliver of a second,
the stranger's body seemed a host
to something else—
and Abraham, astonished,
saw what it was:

a locust, turned away, benign,
its wings dark in the sun—
and then the stranger turned again,
and looked full at Abraham,
as if to see what he had learned.

It made him dizzy then;
it made him dizzy now, to think

of it: yet all he'd thought
before, had turned again, as if
his mind had been a wing.

Isaac

My father was my god.
What he contained, God contained.

My earliest memory is of sacrifice.
My mother, moving slowly, carried the organs
of a lamb to the small shrine.
The smell of their burning sickened me,
yet made me hungry
for her breast.

I don't remember
much of my childhood.
When my mother died,
she whispered to me,
"You are the vessel."
I asked her what she meant,
but she only smiled.
I moved closer to her because she was weak,
and asked her again, "For what?"
But she only smiled a sad soft smile,
looking at me and beyond me.
I asked her a third time, "What do I contain?"
but my mother did not breathe again.

I have seen that sad smile
on the faces of women,
have longed to know what they know,
what they contain.
I saw that sad smile on the lips of my wife,
and I told her what I was thinking.
But Rebekah drew back from me,
her eyes unbelieving,
her lips no longer soft.
She said, "Do what a man does, Isaac."
After that night we would not again
lie down as husband and wife.

Now I am an old man,
yet I remember so clearly
that mountainside, the single tree,
the harsh cry of the ram.

Something glittered in my father's hand
like a wing,
and I had the thought
that I was the ram's better part.
I was its spirit, and I lived.

Rebekah

"The locust is the Lord.
The locust is the scouring Face.
The locust is the scourge of *Elohim*."

Each night before we broke bread
we bowed our heads and spoke
this prayer. One night I peeked
and I swear the old man looked
like a locust himself—glittering, green,
black with rhapsody and rage.
He glared right at me, and it was not
Abraham who stared out, but
some desert creature not a man.

That night I fled from him
inside, gathered my Jacob
to my breast, back to my womb,
if I could, to save him.
We lived inside ourselves
from that day on.

"The locust is the scouring Face."

In dreams I see that old man's face
twisted in the anguish
of his prayer. Those strange, glittering eyes
poke at me, as if a jaw, hidden,
that I'm not quick enough to flee,
follows.

Isaac was a good man,
not filled with rage like his father;
he worried and was kind.
He did not banish me each month,

but walked with me
to the sequestered tent
where I bled.
He visited me during my week;
each day we talked with only
the tent wall between us.
He did not think me unclean.

But we grew old and Isaac cried
out in the night to know
who he was, where he belonged,
in the world the Elohim had promised.
I told him this is the world—
one night he looked at me,
and it was his father's face I saw.
Those strange eyes that frightened me
glittered in the darkness of Isaac's face:
"The locust is the scourge of Elohim"—
intoned, not spoken.

I cried, sobbing his name: "Isaac . . . "
I trembled, begged him to relent.
"The locust is the Lord.
My father is my God."

Esau was his; Jacob mine.
I bear no guilt for my trickery.

The Greatest Generation

Sometimes he looks across America—
he never turns his television off—
and wonders where the country he "fought for"
has "gone." *Gone gone gone, my baby's gone
gone gone,* I hum as I pick up the cue
in the basement of his assisted living.
My daughter asks can we play one more game
before we have to see Moppy and Poppy?
Maybe, I nod, already tense with duty.

Where is the selflessness that drove him
on his knees across a carrier deck,
the shrapnel clanging in the steel above,
to search a stump that was a crewman's leg
seconds before—"Those arteries can slip—
I lost it twice, had to stick my hand up
there a couple times"—the white ball smacks
the colorful wedge with a pleasing sound.
My daughter says breaking takes too much force.

Another time a *kamikaze* struck:
it turned a square steel hallway below decks
into a perfect cylinder of steel.
I held his body—his best friend's body—
his name was Jimmy. . . . My name. The orange ball
rockets toward the side pocket, goes *thunk.*
"Wow, Dad," my baby says, "you're good." She calls,

"Eight ball, corner pocket," then drops it in.
I chase her to the elevator door.

To understand you must go back, always back.
When I was eight, I found a photograph
at Grandma's house—his mother's house: a boy
of eight sat on the dirt floor of a shack.
He looked so much like me, I tried to think
when I'd been there—and who had taken it—
I was so sure I was that other boy.
It was my father who stared back at me:
1930. St. Mary's, Ohio.

Silent, we stand in elevator mode;
its doors stay open longer for wheelchairs,
for those swinging on crutches or walkers.
When it closes, I leap to my daughter,
tickle her while she screams, until the first
floor tone sounds; then we straighten up, blank-faced,
as two old ladies climb aboard, chirping
of bridge. On two, they leave, the heavy door
slides shut. I leap to tickle, as she screams.

He wonders where the country he fought for
has gone. Where is the selflessness that drove
him on his knees across a carrier deck
with shrapnel clanging in the steel above,
to search a stump that was a crewman's leg
moments before, and clamp an artery,
until a doctor could break free and help.

Another time, a *kamikaze* struck,
turning a square steel hallway below decks

into a perfect cylinder of steel;
he held his friend's body, lifeless, concussed.
In 1968, he asked his son,
"But would you go if it was like my war?"
My war, your war, let's give the sons a war . . .
His son was named for that friend he had held.
To understand, you must always go back.
At eight, his son found an old photograph:
a boy of eight sat on a shack's dirt floor.

Of course it was his father who stared back.
There was no humor in that shack, or love.
The mother made clear she deserved "better,"
and when the country crashed, blamed her husband;
that father labored with his arms and back.
There was a tree stump out the kitchen door.
She'd use it to axe chicken necks on days
when there were chicken necks to axe, then rinse
and dry the tool, and hang it on the wall.

One thing about that axe: she kept it sharp.
She had respect for what could get things done.
One afternoon the son came home all bruised.
His teacher at the one-room school caught him
smoking near the building, took a rubber hose,
beat him badly across his arms and back.
She took the axe down, walked two miles to school,

to where the man sat grading at his desk,
and drove the blade into the fleshy wood.

She vowed she would cut off his hand next time,
if he raised it again, against her own.
"It was the only time she ever took my part."
Her grandson came to think, *Not even then:*
It was her own part she took up that day.
A shack is like a cave, part of the land,
the seam between what's in and what's kept out.
His grandfather married a Cherokee;
his black hair, high cheekbones, recalled this love.

He shot and skinned his food, offered rabbits,
squirrels and birds, to the pot of greens each night;
bullets cost a nickel apiece in town.
He swam St. Mary's lake naked, played cards
and dice with St. Mary's boys, went to war.
The ones who owned the country grew concerned
because a *doppelgänger* ran amok
in Europe—seed sprung from their own greed,
and Europe's greed, the son come home to roost.

War's just protection of portfolios.
The ones at desks always sound the alarm;
the ones with high cheekbones, black hair, answer.
The ones at home salute, pretend they know,
manipulate the trade that follows war;
the ones who do the least remain intact.
The others, like abused sons, fall in step.

He swam St. Mary's lake naked, played cards.
Freud said to go forward, you must go back.

Each night he'd leave his family for the "corner":
a room where Yid and Wop and Jap and he
clashed over cards. Pinochle, poker, gin.
On Saturdays he'd drive to the horse tracks—
he called his race track bets a second job.
Sometimes he made his son come with him, cheer.
He wanted to be close, though on his terms;
but to the boy it seemed like servitude,
feelings that deepened Sunday afternoons,

as he chased dice across the bedroom rug,
calling out their numbers through blue air,
to his father, smoking, marking a pad.
They picked him up one night, during the war,
the MPs did—he was drunk, throwing bricks
from some construction site right through the plate-
glass windows of Seattle's finest stores.
They put him in a straitjacket when he
resisted—taunted him, threw him in "the hole."

The drinking didn't stop until the night
in 1960, when his son was twelve;
he took off all his clothes and tried to leave.
His wife, a small woman made big by fear,
wrestled him out of the front door. He slept
nude on the couch, and woke, a naked mirror:
that day he gave up cigarettes and beer,

but kept the ponies and the all-night cards.
Years later he would tell his son his truth:

"Find the vice that keeps you alive, live it."
The other adage his son would remember:
"Hitler was right, but he was immoral."
The son wondered: because he liked to watch
Eva Braun shit? Or was it just the Jews?
But he got it. The code a father sends
his first son is more powerful almost
than any mammal code—it can rival
the one a fetus learns within the womb.

A shack is like a cave, part of the land.
Of course, it was his father who stared back.
Freud said to go forward you must go back.
They all picked up on this: Joyce, Valery.
Two thousand years ago man's spirit split
from limbs and testicles, shoulders and heart;
no longer were the entrails read by those
familiar with the viscera, the whole.
The half-men do the least, return intact.

When he returned, the jobs and housing scarce,
he lived with his parents, and his new wife.
He drank, played cards—pinochle, poker, gin—
sleeping the binges off on pool tables.
His mother hid the key to the bedroom,
would stick her head in several times each night.
If planes flew over while they slept, he'd throw

his wife down on the floor first, cover her.
They had a son, and found a place at last.

One night while they were out, the landlord let
himself into their rooms to look around.
When they returned they found a note that read:
"Your one-year-old has scribbled on my walls!"
He pulled his shotgun from the closet shelf,
went downstairs to the landlord's place, and propped
both barrels under that man's quaking chin.
"Don't *ever* sneak into my home again."
Three days later, the family got the boot.

Sometimes he looks across America,
and wonders "where the country I fought for
has gone." Where is the selflessness that drove
him on his knees across a carrier deck,
with shrapnel singing in the steel above,
to search a stump that was a crewman's leg
moments before, and grip an artery,
until a doctor could break free and help?
A shack is like a cave, part of the land.

There was a tree stump out the kitchen door.
The sky was clear when the *kamikaze* struck,
turning a square steel hallway below decks
into a perfect cylinder of steel:
he held his friend's body, lifeless, concussed.
In 1968, he asked his son,
"But would you go if it was like my war?"

My war, your war, let's give the sons a war . . .
His son was named for that friend he had held.

III

Hand

The machine in which his hand
shredded before his eyes,
until he took a penknife
and severed the remaining flesh,

whirred to the whim of another,
distant machine.

Freud

Come to think of it, I never speak of Mom
much now, though I go on and on about Dad.
My generation's given "Mom" a beating,
I think: there's no son who hasn't got his gun
out for the old dear—the dear in the headlights!
Think it could be, like, you know, like—*Freud?*

Speaking of beatings, who's taken more than Freud,
lately? From the belly of "The Beast," not Mom's:
Shtand ze kike against zer vall! Aim ze headlights! . . .
But why beat Freud instead of dear old Dad?
Dad's the one who's always pulling out his gun,
longing to give *someone* a "Christian" beating!

Freud got a few things wrong—that's worth this beating?
Let's whack some Christians instead of poor Freud.
It's clear they understand about "The Gun"—
but what about "The Cave"? No, no, not Mom's—
and let's not even go there about Dad's.
Their *zeitgeist* is a scramble toward headlights—

figures projected on a wall by headlights—
then, once there, instituting someone's beating.
How do you break it to your "real-life" Dad
that twenty centuries of this *schadenfreude*
are too much? That this smokescreen called "Mom"
just hides the cave of God-Our-Daddy's gun?

They co-opt Jesus into their hired gun—
that rabble-rousing Jewish kid, with head lice—
then claim he cut this strange deal with *his* Mom?
And he'll *return*—to give the "sons" a beating?
No wonder we're devouring poor old Freud!
We'll swallow any tale "revealed" by "Dad."

"I can sell you *anything!*" My own dad
points his shaking finger like a gun
at me. He wonders who the hell is Freud;
He winks and elbows me about "headlights."
His diaper leaks. His pride takes a beating.
I shoo him off to Florida with "Mom."

Amerika: a graveyard, a Mom-and-Dad
beating. Whistle past. Switch on your headlights.
A gun can *be* a gun, even for Freud.

Wars of Nutrition

*In late November [1864] the War Department had
done its part by lowering the minimum standard
height for recruits to "five feet, instead of five feet
three, as heretofore."*

—Shelby Foote, *The Civil War: A Narrative*

The graves show ancient heroes were small men.
Achilles, four feet six, tops. Ajax stood
a towering four feet nine—it must have seemed
he blotted out the sky. Odysseus,
that wily warrior, reached four feet four;
and Nestor, he of counsel grave and wise,
a full four feet—but only if he wore
his battle sandals with the wedges in them.
It's clear small men desire to be large men.
History is the record of small men,
the fabrications of old yarns that made
small men seem big. Size counts, the stories say.

On the set of the newest action flick,
Let's Roll Around In Something Dead Today,
the director is talking to his star.
"Bruce, the car flips over several times,
then like a miracle lands clean and starts.
It's crumpled, and it's wobbly, but you *drive.*
You turn to Tom and smile, 'I've got your back.'"
The star's brow furrows. "Flips several times?"
The other man says patiently, "Don't fret

about the car. Ted'll take care of that.
He's got his fireproof suit." "His fireproof suit?"
"Bruce, how's a cold one sound, till we call the scene?"

Adolf Hitler was short enough to watch
the roughage he fed Eva Braun bear fruit.
Hercules was a stump. His stables tale
has the smell of truth about it—job, not myth.
Six hundred years on, Homer was a *mensch*,
all four feet three of him, blind as a bat.
He moved his players in and out of scenes
just like a good director might today.
"Achilles, you sulk! Don't quit your tent. What?
I said *sulk*—you know I said *sulk!* Nestor,
talk to him? Cassandra, don't be a bitch!
Has anyone seen Hector yet this morning?"

He likely had a couple of assistants
to block out scenes, take care of entire "books"—
perhaps one with a singular talent
for solitary existential throes
was put in charge of spears ripping out eyes,
and long swords maiming leather-sporting groins.
In any case, he celebrated deaths
that happened many centuries before,
reverberating in his "modern" mind—
and yet removed enough for smaller men
to swell their heads with someone else's deeds,
while they reclined and ate a bit of lamb.
It's clear they couldn't scale the walls of Troy:

their ladders were too short, the rungs too close
together, lengths too disproportionate
for easy toting by those pint-sized arms.
Halfway across the field, the top would dip
and topple forward to the bloody earth.
The extra who was carrying it was lost,
ground under heels by fighters as they fled.
The answer took ten years to dawn, of course:
the tiny men could fit inside . . . a *horse!*
Sniggering, they left it near the gate,
then scampered to their tents, to fart and wait.

Back on our movie set, the cameras roll;
the wind machine, nicknamed "Iphigenia,"
swirls some dust around the dented car.
Bruce smirks at Tom, whispers, "I got your *butt!*"
The two crack up; Tom makes some farting sounds
with both his hands. "Cut! Cut!"—the filming stops;
the crew pretends to grin and horse around.
These five-feet-eight-inch symbols of our need
to pose as bigger men than what we are
transfix us in the adolescent dark.
An actress once swore her divorce was "great"—
now she could wear high heels instead of flats.

Anchises

The Don is dead! Long live the Don!
Except there is no more Don, no
succession. He has exited the way he lived:
ripping out his catheter twice, raging,
finally restrained by leather.
In those cuffs he must have seemed
the angry god brought low
to his children, who once bowed
their own heads before his fury.

I didn't hate him, though I should have,
what he did to his daughter, my wife.
What he did to me, through her,
the hidden, even from herself, distrust.
But I didn't have to judge him.
I wasn't the son who, approaching
his fiftieth year, had to remember
not to help, not to offer, anything—
straightening next to the Volvo's trunk,

dismissed by a thoughtless remark
meant only to elbow him away,
shove the man still boy, always boy,
out of the range of kingly notice,
lest he trip the sluice of feeling . . .
I watched the son, my friend now
of thirty years, bow down, not from

new injury or old grievance,
but from the need to carry the old man's

heart . . . Aeneas strapped his father
to his back, my friend's sister, Don's daughter,
my wife, would remember when the fires
flickering through Troy replaced
the bloody catheter in her mind's eye,
and we spread the flag the VA gave us
over the coffin like a cooling cloth.

The Snipers

I read a book about snipers in war,
the ones in World War Two, then Vietnam.
I told myself it was the craft of it
that struck me so—almost an art, it seemed:
the careful calibration of an art.

I mentioned this quite harmlessly—I thought—
at church one picnic barbeque in May.
I've always been a bit insensitive—
I'll talk about abortions while the plates
pile high with sticky meat, that sort of thing—

and my ex-wife would wonder at the rage,
the "animosity," she thought my jokes
revealed. Or hid. I just like the absurd—
we take our pleasures too much for granted;
the mix of dark and light seasons a life.

But none of this came into play that noon.
You notice no one bites when you poke them?
But when your need to get under their skin
is hidden, even from yourself, they'll hit
harder than one of Hemingway's big trout?

The point is—I would tell my wandering wife,
if she were here—I didn't know that John
and Caleb fought as snipers in their wars.

Fact is, I barely know Caleb and John
at all, forget about the guilt they bear;

so when I settled at the picnic table,
balancing my plate of ham, baked beans,
potato salad, and a Heineken,
I had no clue I'd sent them off again
on some forced march they weren't strangers to.

"You've always used the fact I did my job
as proof that I lacked something in my heart."
(My mention of that book while we'd waited
in line for food had started up a talk
I now plopped down right in the middle of.)

"And only you would say it was a job
to watch the melon of a man's head
fly apart." This last was said too strong,
and talk around the edges of us paused;
a child's cry like a shot came through too loud

from the soccer field down the grassy hill.
The old man shifted glumly on the bench.
"You ask a one of us, he'll say the same—
hell, the dead at Normandy'd say the same—
it *was* a job. We made it through that way."

"No snipers hit the beach at Normandy."
"You think we didn't die there, anyway?"
"You didn't, though, did you? Die, I mean."

"Lucky for you," the old man laughed, and drank.
The younger man was old himself. "Lucky,"

he said, lifting his own beer in a toast.
"War's war. They're all alike. You crap your pants,
you freeze, you shake all over, if you live.
And if you don't, you never shake again."
"Or crap." The old man laughed harshly, "Or crap."

Then he paused. "I never was afraid of death.
I was afraid"—he paused again—"of dying."
I saw there was something between them,
for when the father said this, the son's face
for the first time let it all go, almost

as if the two of them had drifted back
to feelings none could feel who walked around
this picnic drinking beer. Caleb faltered, "God—"
"Oh, spare me—what's God got to do with it?
God's what most people substitute for thought—

the only higher power is *yourself*.
Grow up, Caleb. You're sixty-two. It's time."
For all his words' bravado, the old man
had spoken them at cost. His frame seemed spent;
his hands shook as he lifted up his drink.

Right there I started to believe my wife.
I'd wandered into this one, no fault of mine;
and yet I hungered to see where it led.

Even if it meant the old man dead,
and Caleb grinning, dancing on his grave.

"Your war was in the trees, just like my own.
You picked the enemy apart, like me;
you made the choice who lived or died, like me.
Sometimes when I got some poor fool sighted,
I swear I'd feel you pumping through my veins.

I'd feel it was your sight along the barrel,
your heart I had to stop before I fired.
You know the drill. Release a breath, then pull.
I'd see your face before the bullet hit."
There, he'd said it. I hardly dared to drink.

My wife was right—this *is* what I live for:
to stir the pot and see who acted out.
I had the feeling what they both revealed
was just the latest chapter in a book;
and neither one was looking for an end.

The old man rolled his eyes at me, and grinned.
"I eat their food. It's not the worst to sit
amongst them, on a sunny afternoon.
But it's a long, long way to their belief."
I grinned myself. The soccer game was loud.

"I tried to be your friend. I always tried—"
Caleb raised his beer—"to be your friend."
Sometimes this life just isn't long enough

to say what must be said. Or can be said.
In any case, no more was said that day.

November 22, 1963

1

I sat in Miss Reynolds' biology class
the day we all remember what we were doing.
I seem to recollect dissecting a fetal pig;
but perhaps, like Vardaman, I only conflated
physical and metaphysical horror
in one obliterating flash. Probably,
recalling myself as student and young man,
I sat there quietly, watching the others
poke, carve, discover. But at 1:30,
when the intercom coughed without preamble,
and we listened in growing fear to what
resembled a phone conversation broken into
by mistake (ellipses of questioning; sobs;
once, a loud shout) turn slowly into
the focused statement that went through
each of us like a bullet—that he had, in fact,
been murdered—we all sat up & still
then, the radiant pigs forgotten forever.

2

Who can explain the oracular impulse?
That day, they told us to "vacate the premises";
no shoulder to cry on in those spare times; no counsel.
The Phys Ed teachers and the coaches, who would pull boys
from the hallway scrum, and slam their backs against

the walls to make a point, stood there sullen, sour,
as we filed past, silent, not even allowed
to use the phones—but then, who would we have called?
There was a strip mall off the high school lot;
we'd meet there at the bakery before class,
the rich kids in the restaurant nearby.
That day we wandered aimlessly along the storefronts;
what I remember most is our stunned silence.
In a television store I saw
a woman clerk who looked the way
I felt. I blurted out, "We'll never get past this"—
I could feel the fear distort my voice,
as if I knew. She stared at me, as if I knew.

3

Miss Reynolds had good bones, as the connoisseurs
of beauty say, but wore so much make-up she seemed
a mannequin or doll. Or Lady Elaine Fairchilde,
on Fred Rogers' TV show, or Punch's wife, Judy—
an alabaster reach of flesh in which soft
eyes seemed trapped. I've often wondered since
if she was the first transsexual I'd known,
her perfect over-lipsticked lips a truth some
lonely man pined for in his own mirror.
I was fifteen: desire needed no abyss.
Even wrinkled old Mrs. Benedict—
even hoary old Mrs. B—would writhe beneath me
in my bed at night, while I sucked her ancient
leathery nipples, and groaned aloud.

I wasn't rich or president;
the Beatles had yet to play on Ed Sullivan;
RFK was still alive, like me.
And everywhere I looked, desire fused with death.

Brunch with Sonny Liston

Four years later, in the coffee shop of the
Thunderbird Hotel, I'm having brunch with Sonny
Liston . . .

—Jerry Izenberg

What's this? Salmon? My mom made salmon cakes,
Fridays. Flattened them like hamburgers, fried
them in a skillet, but nothing like this—you sure
it's fresh, man? I guess I use the fork that's in it?

My own fork's not good enough, right? Maybe some
black man saliva gets on a white guy's salmon?
He'd die, right? He'd die if a little drop of my spit
got mixed up with his? My spit would drop him?

No, I don't want any rolls, man. Thanks. Carbs.
I'm coming back, you know. Picking up a paycheck
or two, is all. Not challenging Mr. Big Mouth, no.
I know the score. I was the Right Negro, for a while,

then all of a sudden I'm the Wrong Negro—right?
I'm *too* scary. You ought to look into *your* mirror
some morning, you want scary. I lost that fight.
Nat Fleischer says I lost it, so I lost it, right?

Who told you the brothers threatened my family—
I never said that! The only profit I got use for

is the kind you put in the bank, but I never
said that. Yeah, they was yelling about my gloves.

No, you have some. It don't look like toast to me.
And what's "French" about it? Thanks for getting
these scrambled, by the way. I didn't know you
could ask. I hate eggs look like Sambo eyes.

So some cut shit got on his eyes—so life's tough!
I got to watch out for every fucking brother?
Is that jam any good? Maybe I will have a roll.
All that boy did was talk talk talk. And dance:

he stands still, he's laid out on a stretcher, man.
I'm telling truth. How's he get to be everybody's
hero? Fool don't even serve. I don't mind
the Muslim shit—I never said they leaned on me!

I can get dessert, too? They make me a sundae,
you think? Vanilla, man, lots of chocolate sauce,
if you don't mind. And whipped cream, nuts—
and a cherry? I'm like a kid with sundaes, man.

I don't want to talk about the mob. I be killing
Kennedy, before you're through. Don't know
nothing about no "Mob," okay? Never killed
nobody. Except you, maybe, you keep pushing.

Now this is good. Tasty. Smooth. How come
white ice cream's tastier than brown ice cream?

No opinion? Seems unnatural, don't it? Maybe
Negroes be tired of eating stuff that's brown?

Don't have nothing to say about no Mob! Not
connected, never been. And I don't do drugs—
I don't like needles, man! It's Mama Whiskey,
and her girl, Sugar, the ones'll take me down.

That's all me and him got in common, man—
you know, before the glove man tape your hands,
they stick that deadener in you—me and him,
we're the only ones won't let them stick us.

You find me dead with a needle next to me,
they got to me, man. *Who?* I don't know who!
Not the Mob, not the brothers—you find me dead,
it was *life*, man. Life did me in. "A man's

a man, for all that." My mom used to read me
poems. I done what I had to do. . . . You picking
this up? Thanks, man. You're not so bad, Jerry,
for a honky with a paunch. Yeah, I'll have a mint.

The Pursuit of Happiness

She tells Don he can suck her nipple rings—
the trouble is, the leakage hasn't stopped.
Her blouse—she never wears a bra—is soaked;
the suppuration's milky, and yet fine . . .
Don blushes, holds a palm up: "Rain check."

After the murderer had served ten years,
he had one skill: tattoos. In his kitchen,
he gave her bourbon, leather, went to work.
She sits here now, envelope of color,
a bright tableau of birds, snakes, one word: *Cunt.*

"I'm sick of typing memos for you guys!"
Don worries that they'll find someone as good.
He leafs through snapshots of a "dungeon"
some fool has built for her in hot L.A.
"I need to be stretched out upon *that* cross . . . "

She claims he'll make her beg, on her tiptoes,
at least a day before he lets her come.
She goes on how the sounds he'll make her make
will match the colors leaping on her skin.
Don worries that they'll find someone as good.

Famous Poet Visit

Before the public illness of his wife
(which they'd both milked the last years of her life)
had left her body moldering and cold,
he was boffing a twenty-six-year-old,
and eager to reveal details at dinner.
Her beauty's like my dick, he leered—*it's inner.*

A young man thought, Old Man, I got your *inner*—
but not because he cared about the wife;
that wasn't why he pushed away his dinner.
He'd had a sudden vision of *his* life:
he was another twenty-six-year-old—
the thought of old male flesh had left him cold.

He let the food he couldn't eat grow cold.
He watched the old fool's outer turn to inner.
Though he *was* only twenty-six years old,
he got how solipsism and a wife
make such a one a rich repast of life—
and *faux love* a sweet brandy after dinner.

"Monsieur, you are finished with your dinner?"
Above the plate, the waiter's eyes were cold.
He nodded, flinching from that show of life—
yet one more outer letting slip an inner.
The plate vanished. He conjured up the wife,
when she was only twenty-six years old—

was this old fart ever twenty-six years old?
Had they played footsie underneath their dinner?
Warmed each other's flesh against the cold?
He mused upon the illness of the wife:
was Death the lover with his dick in her?
Could dying *be* the living of a life?

"Dessert, Monsieur?" He leaned back into life,
what they were calling life, tonight. The old
boy's elbow plied him. "Get it? '*Inner*'?
'In *her*'?" He smiled weakly. Maybe his wife
had sometimes smiled like this, over dinner,
when her revulsion left her body cold.

The old man loved a twenty-six-year-old,
who had something of his dead wife in her.
Life can be cold. And cheat you out of dinner.

Sporting Life

Wilt Chamberlain
discovered sin
required a log,
to log them in.

❖

Pete Rose, brother,
by any other
moniker would stink,
is what I think.

◆

Joe DiMag
ruled like the Raj.
But when he passed,
they capped his ass.

Tiresias

You learn how to be a man from your father.
Your mother teaches you how to be a woman.
You have to fear becoming an old man
before you'll take on the wiles of the mother—
her movements, gestures, the way her face
suddenly, at odd moments, becomes your face.

Turns out the old adage about saving face
was really about saving the face of the father.
His was the look you wanted on your face
whenever you'd realize you were a woman.
Those moments shocked you—and your mother,
who'd assumed you'd turn out to be a man.

But it's not that you haven't ended up a man:
mornings you shave, staring into a man's face;
you have the proper attitude toward your mother.
You just don't want to be a man like your father,
and the best way to do that is to be a woman.
The first time you saw this happen in your face,

it scared you: Your hand flew up to your face.
Not only did you have the cunning of a man,
now you also had the guile of a woman.
You look into the mirror at your new face,
one begun the night it surprised your father,
humping a blanket that turned into your mother.

How could the bastard do that to your mother?
And why had you never seen this in her face?
What was it you saw next day in your father?
A look that told you he was the better man?
And what do you think he saw in your face?
Did he know then that you were a woman?

You repressed that morning in the way a woman
might repress an impractical love for a man.
When he's around, you can see it in her face—
her *Don't-trust-him-but-still-love-him* face.
Your father never thought of you as a man.
It was natural you'd try to seduce your father.

First you showed your father your "mother" face;
but then you showed him your other face,
the sly face a man wears when he's a woman.

IV

The War of All Against All

They come in through the porous basement walls.
They're so quick, you only get one shot;
I make it count. I couldn't sleep, to know
I'd missed, and vermin ran free in the walls.
They're like a thought—undisciplined, overt—

that slips out from the heart, vertiginous,
careening, yet alive with shame and doubt.
They're like a thought of love someone must kill,
to keep its freedom safe from running free—
a love that festers in the heart, unsaid.

I understand the hunter in the night.
The hunter needs the moment when the flesh
becomes spirit; he breathes it in, a dark
knowing, inhales it almost like a drug:
the spirit that redeems unspoken love.

He thought he was a darkness I would fear;
his teeth shone in the gloom. He held his knife
as if he meant to put it on display,
to make such presentation magnify
my sense of those few seconds I had left:

he longed to see me paralyzed with fear.
I understand the need to kill, that joy.
That one communion runs so deep in us,

we have to spout the opposite to live;
we hide its need in altered looks and words.

He meant to make me watch my coming death.
It's odd the way the brain protects itself;
fear was a pathway clean enough to trap:
paralysis, horror, my limbs too slow
to get away; yet wide-eyed enough

to watch myself be murdered on the floor.
Fear was a possibility, a death—
it sharpened me, made my movements taut.
But a different primal force surged up,
and I was back in that newspaper shed,

and we were boys, and some boy thought he knew
the boy I was, and what he'd do to me.
We wrestled every Wednesday, after school,
before the truck came with the papers.
We settled scores among us, fought

whatever symbols made us weak: we fought
to ravel out the anger hid in us.
I didn't have the size of other boys,
but I was quick, strong with a tensile strength;
my arms were thin as wires, but like wires

they coiled and locked. I knew to let weight
fly past me, let the ground or wall absorb
the blow. To stay in close, and move—to pull,

or get his arm behind his back, and push—
and if he wouldn't let up, flick an eye.

Most boys devise a reason to retreat,
when they realize it won't be you who stops.
I broke a boy's arm once. He was so big,
but way too soft—he thought he'd sit on me.
He had a style he'd learned from the TV;

I saw it in his eyes across the room:
he thought he'd crush me like a cockroach.
He came out wild, but I ducked down, grabbed;
his fists fell on my back like heavy rain.
He lost balance; I rose up so his back

couldn't protect his head, which slammed the floor.
He shouted out, angry. Surprised and hurt,
he tried to roll, but left his arm exposed;
I pushed it up behind his back as far
as it would go, until I heard it snap.

The way he looked at me when it was done—
astonishment, and horror, too, and fear—
the pain had made him be a boy again.
But this one was a man, not a fat boy.
Because I stared, he faltered, tried to see

what my eyes were saying about his eyes:
He tries to kill himself by killing me.
We understand these things without the words.

I saw fear leap from me back into him.
He had the knife, but now because mistake

was dangerous, he couldn't court mistake:
he had to swing the knife, though off-balance,
alarmed at levels too deep for his thought.
He swung it viciously; I saw the hate
replace the grin: now fear of viciousness

would do me in. The sheer power of thrust
would knock me cringing back against the wall;
and he would follow with a second thrust.
But I had seen that trace of fear, and he
had seen I'd seen. I took him from his dream,

and put him in another dream, my dream.
Son of a bully, I could bully, too:
I'd wait it out, pretend that I was weak;
and when they went too far, let fly, fury
of some betrayal searing up in me.

I saw in their recoil astonishment—
the quick insight that what had started this
wasn't what fueled it now. But that would pitch
my fury and my sense of right higher,
and higher still, until I turned their strength

against them, like a lever I could pull,
inflicting pain with small movement. I don't
know how the others fought; I fought to win.

It was a hesitation I played for,
a stumble slight enough, a second lost.

His eyes showed me, before he swung the knife,
the arc was aiming for my neck. I leaned back
just enough, didn't stumble, grabbed the pipe—
the plumbing pipe exposed above my head—
swung into him with all the force in me.

I caught him at the one instant he had
least purchase on the earth; the knife slipped free.
I didn't need it: when he fell, his head
broke open on a sharp brick in the wall.
But I picked up the knife, pulled his neck back,

and slit it like a pig's. You get one shot;
you better make it pay. His eyes opened
on mine again; I let him see my eyes.
This time, I let him look full in my eyes . . .
No one is going to understand my life.

I don't say that because I feel unique;
in fact, opacity is daily bread;
passion lifts us above the daily ruse.
It's someone else's dream, that we can know
each other. But nearly knowing's the base

we build a life on, build a world. We think
trading the cards of loneliness is love.
It focuses the energy inside

on a table, two drinks, a beach, a couch;
a drive through rainy streets; a child; a gift.

Whatever gets the other to be *there*—
sharing the inner and the outer world
for just the stretch of time that we require—
the gratitude we feel at those moments
passes for knowing someone to the full.

The irony is this: when we pretend
to know our opposite—when we lie down
and give ourselves to someone else in love—
we transfer our *unknowing* into them.
It's a relief we feel, not ecstasy—

the joy of self-awareness unachieved—
sloughed off in cries of oneness to some god.
There's no recourse: nothing is redeemed.
A woman thinks the universe is hers—
which is to say, the lovely thing she is,

she makes believe is everybody else—
until chance kills her child. Now suddenly,
the sky is rent; the woman's out of time.
And lovely as she is, she thinks the world
still mapped by her coordinates, still feels

the universe itself is out of time.
I welcomed him; I felt the welcome rage
uncurl inside, but not to strut or vaunt,

as his forced him to do in front of me.
I felt what I had felt when I was young;

but now that I was old the rage broke clear,
and nothing bounded it. It was a sea
inside my arms, my legs, my face; it roared.
He must have seen my face, for his face changed;
I think he heard a whisper in his gut

that warned him not to move, but still he came.
I watched his feet; I watched his hands: one slip
was all I needed, all I could expect;
and when it came I had to move inside
the sweep of all he was, gain entry to

the place he took for granted remained sealed.
He wanted me to fall upon his rear,
the way an army or a lover does;
or God, who batters sinners' lonely hearts.
So many of us substitute a dream

somebody else has dreamed for what we want.
Of course that was the source of all his rage:
his actions didn't stem from what he was.
Or rather that they did, but what he was
was what he had become, not what he'd be,

when he lay on the floor, staring at me.
The rage went out of him like air released;
and he was what was left: a memory,

an image from the past; astonishment.
He had no strength to stop me as I grabbed

the knife, and, lifting up, sliced through the neck,
as he had tried before to do to me.
The boy whose arm I broke came back to me;
I suppose on future nights this one
will dart before my eyes again, like love . . .

How could I tell police I breathed him in?
They think it's all so logical, so clear.
His look leaped from hatred to fear, and back;
then he knew the truth: that both were one.
There comes a moment when a man's on keel,

the unpaid debts that worry him behind,
the future dreams that lure him on undreamed:
he can't be beaten in that moment.
He steps free from the dream we dream for him,
and all he is is staring out at you.

He saw I didn't fear the thing he feared.
He saw his dream to make me watch my death
was someone else's dream he had lived out . . .
I don't believe in change, except in death.
How could I tell police I breathed him in?

He found the love he'd searched for all his life—
his eyes let me know this—those loving eyes,
that locked on mine, as life poured out his throat.

I had to breathe him in; I couldn't leave
that spirit running free inside my walls.

V

Blue Shorts

He followed a pair of blue shorts up a mountain once.
Her blue shorts were like a flag,
and he was like a troop of men,
following it to the peak.

When they got to the top, they looked out;
it was, of course, magnificent.
But what did you expect?
They were on the top of a mountain.

Coming back down, she felt dizzy,
so they drove deeper into the mountains,
came to a tourist spot that was almost closing,
ate some small cakes and milk.

When they got home, he kissed her ass,
licked her pussy from behind,
then she got on top of him and they fucked,
until she tugged the base of his penis,

and he came, screaming into her shoulder
to muffle the cry, and she came
more quietly, making small sounds
against his chest. Night covered them.

Her blue shorts were crumpled in a corner;
his pants lay alongside the bed.

The morning stretched like a mountain lion around them, guarding the innocents as they slept.

Ross

I think of the ones who've had
a death sentence read to them,
like my friend Ross who suffered

non-Hodgkins lymphoma early
and soaked in so much radiation
he would discover in his forties

only one in two who'd endured
such remedy lasted past fifty.
When he told me of the studies,

I swore he'd be in the good half,
but neither of us believed it;
he shook his head no, smiling.

I sat with others at his funeral,
staring at the simple pine box,
thinking of the worlds—the words—

we came from, and of my own end,
the box awaiting me—no doubt,
an ornate Catholic above-ground

denial of the feast-day to follow;
his box gave something of his voice.
How can a Brooklyn Jew, I'd ask,

and a lapsed Mick from the sticks,
have anything to talk *about?*
Ross would laugh his cranky,

delighted laugh, and call me
some mocking name in Yiddish.
Once, after he made me capitalize

the word "God" in a poem,
I swore I'd never suffered from,
or basked in the whoop-de-do of,

a single day of faith in my life.
"So maybe you don't believe"—
as I smiled—"but He might exist

for someone else, you know."
"You have a point," I say, "though,
you part your hair a certain way,

no one will notice." Then I paled
for his lost hair. "This is why I
love you," he cried. "You *schlemiel!*"

Buying a Dog for Margaret

Sometimes a door swings open,
like a mask from a face,
and to do no harm,
to be allowed to do no harm,
to those we love,
is the greatest gift we can be granted;
and what was will not be again,
the greatest truth and sorrow.

My daughter asks for a dog.
It seems such a humble request
in the great scheme of things,
a desire expressed each day by thousands,
maybe millions of children,
and turned down by millions of fathers,
who have other things to love.

But I wake in the night to the thought
that we can never revisit, undo.
Others would call it a recurring nightmare,
this panic that revisits me
so often, this great blackness, this door
that swings open like the emptiness of a face,
showing me all that can't be redeemed—

the fields, the grasses of the earth, the suns
that were so much more powerful

than the thought of myself on those days,
which are all blackness, darkness, now.

And I am so grateful, so pathetically grateful,
to be awakened to this terror,
to be brought close in dreams to voices
that speak again only at this price;
and the question is, as it has always been,
who or what has awakened me?

In a dream, Margaret's lips
stumble against the side of my face
as she whispers in my ear her urgency:
Please understand, you who have all the power,
I need a dog. Not just want, but need.

And what awakens me tells me
all I have not lived, all I have not redeemed,
will be as nothing in the future,
if I don't honor this need of hers to love.

Dog

We truncate what you need to be
to fit you in your lucky life
with us. We cut and paste, to see
the version that brings us delight.

The almost-language in your eye,
that seems such sorrow to my own,
is just a suffocated cry
that leaves you, finally, alone,

and willing to accept much less:
a place beside the hearth, had we
still hearths; mock food; a pedigree
that shapes, yet won't admit, redress.

My Father's Rope

My father packed a rope into every suitcase
when he went out to all the wooden towns
after the war, offering his wares.
Each suitcase was made of cardboard,
like all the other suitcases
of the men offering America's wares
after the war, the necessary war.
"All those hotels were made of wood,"
he told me once, cunning and fear
I'd come to know in him at war
in his face. "The Allegheny, the old Fairfax
in Wheeling, the Dexter, pride of Fremont, Ohio.
I'd call ahead; sometimes I had to call
more than a month ahead, to book a room
that wasn't higher than the second floor.
Fire took 'em all—yeah, every single one
burned down. I'd been to war, I wasn't going to fry
on a fourth-floor ledge. I packed my rope."
Standard-issue clothesline, doubled back,
and tied at three-foot intervals with a knot
they taught him in the Navy, in the war.

Mad Men

Two men walk into a boardroom.
Each one carries a spear; each wears a mask.
Each man is afraid of his own death,
but is no less willing to strike, to rend, kill.
Each mask is a grotesque mirror of rage,
meant to inspire mortal fear;
each man hopes the other will be made
too afraid to fight when he finally
confronts him and his hideous mask.
Each man had a father who told him
his mask represents his true nature within.
Each man had a mother who told him
it represents what he wants other men
to believe about his true nature within.
As young men, each came to accept
his father's version of what his mask means,
so had faith in his mask for many years.
But as he gets older and closer to death,
each wonders if his mother's explanation
might not be the true one, after all.
Either his mask has reflected his true self
all along, or he has turned into his mask.
It becomes increasingly important
to know whether his mother's story
or his father's is the one he can believe.
Neither man betrays doubt as he glares
through the haze his cigarette makes;
doubt gives other men a license to strike.

Yet it's only doubt that allows him
to hold the two versions together
in his mind, in some sort of balance.
Two men walk through a boardroom;
they carry spears, wear fearsome masks.
Each man is afraid, but for all his confusion,
is no less willing to strike, to rend, kill;
and he thinks his father, finally, is right.
But when his face distorts beneath its mask,
and, cursing the other, he hurls his spear,
each man remembers the words of his mother.

Fantasy with Plane

What partner in a timeworn marriage, or any marriage,
watching the other partner get on a plane,
hasn't felt a small window open inside, briefly,
onto an island with soft sunlight in mild air, flowers,
where choices are undone, promises unmade,

and the possibility of new beginnings, new eyes,
may be purchased by just a few seconds of panic—
okay, many minutes of mad terror and awful grief,
actually, followed by excruciating dismemberment,
but over so quickly it can be called instantaneous

in the long view of things—only to have that window
slammed shut by stone hands of guilt that try
to catch one's fingertips under the rocketing wood,
while the plane takes off into its blue certainty
of safety statistics and industry-standard efficiency . . .

Driving back home, a new fantasy opens its arms
like a relative at a funeral—and now she stands
in a drugstore, in the sparkling city she's flown into,
about to buy something that will help her sleep.
The man waiting next to her smiles pleasantly, asks

"Are you with the conference?" and for once
the sunlight pouring through the smudged windows
behind the cash register touches her hair in all

the right places, and the way she lifts her head
and turns to answer him somehow sloughs off

at least a decade of anxiety about money and work,
not to mention the stress of living with someone
who daydreams about her violent, painful death.
And the voice that begins to come out of her
is a voice she hasn't heard in at least a decade,

yet it matches up perfectly with her hair,
so they skip the keynote speech for some dinner,
and later, walking slowly back to the hotel,
he slips his hand gently but decisively into hers,
and suddenly it's all new again, it's all new.

"Some One Invisible"

Jonathan Edwards described Sarah Pierrepont,
when he was twenty and she thirteen:
"She will sometimes go about
from place to place, singing sweetly;
and seems to be always full
of joy and pleasure; and no one knows
for what. She loves to be alone,
walking in the fields and groves,
and seems to have some one invisible
always conversing with her."
Four years later, they married.

So many sing in the fields,
certain someone is watching them
practice their spontaneities.
When I met my younger daughter,
popping her glorious head
out of her mother's eager body,
and falling safely into my hands,
I saw she was filled with a light
that would move her to every window,
every column of air, as a kindred spirit,
not as a metaphor she desired
others to believe about her joy.

Now she is twelve, nearing the puberty
Sarah Pierrepont walked in thrall to,
aware or unaware of the gaze

of stern young Edwards,
who yearned for the autocratic
and the authentic both:
the body and the soul become
the seamless shining One,
singing to itself amid God's grace.

The Leash

Many people work hard in life, not just you.
Many people look down a street, as you do,
thinking, *This is all I'm going to see, the arc*
of working hard has brought me to this street;
any illusion I had that I would be plucked
from this street has clarified like the rings
around a cartoon character's head as it enters
a bell, is struck, then comes out again, ringing:
one ring gradually tightens around the skull.
The streetlights shine precisely down on the cars;
the cars are daubs of color on a canvas
under the moon. And you're standing there,
holding a leash, waiting for the dog to piss.

VI

The Passion

When I build a fire in the living room
and unroll my sleeping bag beside it
it dawns on me I'm not
the outdoors type.
Or perhaps I'm the one who drops,
carelessly, the lighted cigarette,
hurrying down the mountain before rain.
What follows me has found me,
here, in my own house.

Slowly, the fire takes over.
It licks the walls, rings the windows,
defers to the magic circle
I draw with my wife's lipstick.
I sit inside it, watching the floor disappear.
Maybe someone will come
with more water, or more fire.

Moses

i.

In the beginning was a meal and a promise.
There was lamb, crackling in its skin;
there was fruit, olives and grapes, and wine;
and bread, and cheese from goat milk.

There was water that the *Elohim,*
as if he were a man, poured into his hair,
over his wrists and hands, and his face,
flushing away the sand and the sweat

of the desert, and of manhood. The Lord
came to us as a man, and his smile
caused Abraham to believe, and his touch
filled Sarah's ancient womb with life.

What a cagey god, our dear *Elohim,*
bringing to man the fire of an idea.
Not only that we are better than other men,
but that a man is better than a brute.

The Lord no longer calls himself by name.
He makes me to hear his voice,
as if it is my voice, inside my head;
when I look for him, I see only fire.

This voice caused Abraham to raise
a knife against his son; and then
it made an angel to hold back his arm,
seek out the kid bleating with fear.

Lying on that rock, Isaac saw
the lack of pity in his father's eyes;
how does a son sit at a table, share
a meal with such a father, ever after?

ii.

In the beginning was the word and the meal.
We have always been a blend of talk and food.
This was the table on which the words began.

Now I am alone on a dry mountain in a dry desert,
talking to a fire in a tree.
Who am I, that have begun to hear voices?

"They do not know you are the only God,"
I say to this fire.
"But you know," the fire replies.

I know, I know—what do I know?
I know this God's words are graven in my head
as on tablets of stone.

I know he has offered to help, but his price is high.
"When Abraham broke bread with me,

I was not there. I was within him;
I was the thought of himself,
who would be the founder of a great people.
And when he looked at me, he saw an insect."

"When I look at you, I see nothing."

"Believe me," said the fire, "this is a good thing."

iii.

In the desert, in the beginning, was the Word:
the sun, the water, the wine, and the lamb.
The memory of a meal, and the *Elohim's* promise:

musical talk, the tearing of the bread like flesh.
Time is a prison, and yet a flimsy gate.

"They imagined me as a bull.
I need new imaginings."

Somewhere in that desert, the *Elohim*
changed from a bull to a man.
The glory of the change
was to understand the old—the brute in us—
while having faith in the new.

The god we know now
knew then that change must come

at once, but gently, that we might know
his glory and our sons' glory.
My holy land has been the faces
surrounding me, as they began to see
the promise of the sons.

Each man will be his own temple,
lay upon its table
the sacrifice of himself, the brute in him.

And one will come among us,
and we will know him.

Who can know the righteousness
a man feels raising his arm
in the service of the word of God?
Only the elders, whose sons will see
the land he's promised them.

Only the elders carry the Word
inside themselves, as their own.

We have learned
the holes of darkness
in our speech,
that once were prayers.

Time is a prison,
and a flimsy gate.

We know too much to know
this land we are promised,
and not enough.

iv.

I wish I had a friend. Just one good friend.
Instead, I have this unseen God,
who fills me with a righteousness
I bring to others as a fire.

Why has the god of Abraham
forsaken me? Why is a burning tree
all I have left of him who walked
across the desert as a man?

My people fall silent when I approach.
They fear I serve another god,
whose rage resembles my own rage;
they say they fear my righteousness.

v.

"Your people are my people," the fire says.
"You grew from an idea, whispered across a table,
that you were better than other men.

Even if you weren't, you were; for I chose you.
It was time for some men to love me,
to listen to different words and pretend

they were the forgotten ones, now remembered."
Why do we believe in this God?
With Abraham he breaks bread;
with me he breaks my balls.

"You protected my people, my idea.
But you know too much, and too little,
to enter the land I promised you, my son."

"I am not your son."

"For this, too," says the fire, consuming the tree.

vi.

The part of me that wished my father's death
I see reflected in my son,
who wishes mine. The promised land
is honeyed land, absent the fathers,
though the fathers made it so.
We stare across time's gate
at what we can't possess:
a dream in which
the everyday takes place,
the waxing of the ordinary time,

where death is not extinct—
we are not fools—
but where old men watch for generations hence.

Detaching fruit from stem
could take an hour in this land, maybe more:
color, scent, its roundness in the hand.
For many worlds make up the fruit
and all of them
must be lived through
before the glory of its sun can set,
spreading its color throughout the limbs.

That the old man can see the child
his child produces,
and that child's child:
this is the land we were promised.

vii.

What belongs to us
is the desire of the fathers for the sons.
This desire is anywhere the sons flourish,
anywhere we know the sons as sons.

Sometimes on that mountain I thought
it was I who had invented him, the Lord God.
It was I who spoke, dared; it was I.
Is this why I raged at my people?

Soon I will be helpless in the night,
dwindling in the dark, praying for sleep.
I will pray for the cooling hand of sleep.
I will beg the Lord God for sleep.

The Poets March on Washington

What do we want?
Immortality!
When do we want it?
Now!

What do we want?
Immortality!
When do we want it?
Now!

What do we want?
Immortality!
When do we want it?
Now!

Notes

"Sporting Life" makes reference to the tumble Joe DiMaggio's reputation took after his death, when many portrayed him as a narcissistic old skinflint and heartless man.

"Ross" is for the late Ross Feld, novelist, essayist, and poet.

"Some One Invisible" – the quoted material is from Jonathan Edwards' longer passage on his future wife, Sarah Pierrepont, written about 1723, when Sarah was thirteen.

This book is for Richard Howard, mentor and friend.